POINTS OF VIEW

Is the ELECTORAL COLLEGE Necessary?

By Meghan Green

Published in 2021 by
KidHaven Publishing, an Imprint of Greenhaven Publishing, LLC
353 3rd Avenue
Suite 255
New York, NY 10010

Designer: Deanna Paternostro
Editor: Jennifer Lombardo

Photo credits: Cover Jock Fistick/Bloomberg via Getty Images; pp. 5 (main), 21 (inset, middle-right) Rob Crandall/Shutterstock.com; p. 5 (inset) Joe Amon/The Denver Post via Getty Images; p. 7 (main) Win McNamee/Getty Images; p. 7 (inset) Gino Santa Maria/Shutterstock.com; p. 9 (main) warasit phothisuk/Shutterstock.com; p. 9 (inset) pandapaw/Shutterstock.com; p. 11 Mark Ralston/ AFP via Getty Images; p. 13 (top) littlenySTOCK/Shutterstock.com; p. 13 (bottom) Christian Hinkle/ Shutterstock.com; p. 15 Giraphics/Shutterstock.com; p. 17 Henny Ray Abrams/AFP via Getty Images; pp. 19, 21 (inset, left) a katz/Shutterstock.com; p. 21 (notepad) ESB Professional/Shutterstock.com; p. 21 (markers) Kucher Serhii/Shutterstock.com; p. 21 (photo frame) FARBAI/iStock/Thinkstock; p. 21 (inset, middle-left) Andrey_Popov/Shutterstock.com; p. 21 (inset, right) StunningArt/ Shutterstock.com.

Library of Congress Cataloging-in-Publication Data

Names: Green, Meghan, author.
Title: Is the electoral college necessary? / Meghan Green.
Description: New York : KidHaven, [2021] | Series: Points of view | Includes index.
Identifiers: LCCN 2019049071 (print) | LCCN 2019049072 (ebook) | ISBN 9781534534261 (library binding) | ISBN 9781534534247 (paperback) | ISBN 9781534534278 (ebook) | ISBN 9781534534254 (set)
Subjects: LCSH: Electoral college–United States–Juvenile literature.
Classification: LCC JK529 .G72 2021 (print) | LCC JK529 (ebook) | DDC 324.6/3–dc23
LC record available at https://lccn.loc.gov/2019049071
LC ebook record available at https://lccn.loc.gov/2019049072

Printed in the United States of America

Some of the images in this book illustrate individuals who are models. The depictions do not imply actual situations or events.

CPSIA compliance information: Batch #BS20K: For further information contact Greenhaven Publishing LLC, New York, New York at 1-844-317-7404.

Please visit our website, www.greenhavenpublishing.com. For a free color catalog of all our high-quality books, call toll free 1-844-317-7404 or fax 1-844-317-7405.

CONTENTS

What Is the ELECTORAL COLLEGE?

The Electoral College isn't a school. In fact, it isn't a place at all! When people in the United States vote for the president, they're actually voting for electors in their state who will most likely vote for a certain person for president. The number of electors each state gets depends on how many **representatives** that state has in Congress. Then, the electors meet and vote for the president. This process is called the Electoral College.

Some people think the Electoral College is a good way to elect a president. Other people think the United States should get rid of it. Read on to learn more about both sides of this argument!

Know the Facts!

The Electoral College is in the U.S. **Constitution**, so it's the way U.S. presidents have been elected since the country was created.

The votes ordinary citizens cast in an election are called the popular vote. The votes the electors cast are called the electoral vote.

Hard to CHANGE

Some people argue that we should keep the Electoral College because even though it's not perfect, it works. They say any system will have problems, so it doesn't make sense to completely change the way the United States holds elections just because of problems with the Electoral College. Many also say we should keep doing things the way the Founding Fathers wanted.

However, many people who oppose the Electoral College point out that things are different now than when the Constitution was written. These people believe the way U.S. elections work needs to change because the world has changed. For example, **political parties** have changed and grown in modern times.

Know the Facts!

In 1992, Bill Clinton won the presidency with only 43 percent of the popular vote. The other 57 percent was split among his Republican opponent, George H. W. Bush, and **candidates** from smaller parties.

In 2016, Jill Stein ran for president with the Green Party. It's smaller than the main political parties, so she got less attention than candidates such as Bernie Sanders.

Following the FOUNDING FATHERS

One of the reasons why people say we should keep the Electoral College is because the Founding Fathers thought it was a good idea. They thought voters might not always make the best choice. Before the internet, television, and radios were invented, it was hard for people to get news. They might not have known all the important things about candidates when they voted.

Some people think the Electoral College is still needed for this reason. They say that even though we have a lot of ways to look up facts now, many people don't do that. They might vote for someone who isn't a good candidate. If that happens, electors from some states are allowed to vote differently than the people in those states did.

Know the Facts!

Founding Father Alexander Hamilton thought the Electoral College was a good way to make sure the election wasn't controlled by political parties.

The Founding Fathers met at Independence Hall (shown here) to figure out the best way to run their new country. Many of them, including Alexander Hamilton, supported the Electoral College.

Out with the OLD

Some people don't think we need the Electoral College anymore. They say the country has changed a lot since the Constitution was written and voters are better **informed** now.

They also point out that even though the Electoral College was supposed to be fair to everyone, today the electors are often important members of the two main political parties. These two parties are the Democratic and Republican parties. Electors generally vote for the candidate who's in their party, even if they think he or she wouldn't do a good job as president. Some people think this shows that the Electoral College isn't working the way it was supposed to.

Know the Facts!

According to a 2019 **poll**, 72 percent of Democratic voters and 30 percent of Republican voters think the president should be elected based on the popular vote alone.

The 2016 U.S. presidential race between Donald Trump and Hillary Clinton (shown here) showed how divided the country had become along political party lines.

Making It FAIR

People who support the Electoral College say it's the best way for all states to have fair representation. There are many more voters in certain areas of the country, such as big cities. If the Electoral College didn't exist, some people believe, candidates would only have to make promises to the parts of the country that have the most voters. This means people who live in smaller communities wouldn't have their voices heard.

Although the number of electors for each state is based on population, a candidate has to win the electors for an entire state to get that state's vote. This makes it fairer, people say, because candidates have to listen to all voters in every state if they want to win those votes.

Know the Facts!

There are 538 electors total. A candidate needs at least 270 electoral votes to win the presidency.

Many people believe that if the Electoral College didn't exist, presidential candidates wouldn't care about people who don't live in cities.

Opposing SWING STATES

People who oppose the Electoral College say it isn't as fair as it seems. Certain states almost always vote for a certain political party; for example, California and New York almost always vote for a "blue," or Democratic, candidate, while Indiana almost always votes "red," or Republican. This means that candidates often spend more time talking to voters in "swing states," or states that could vote either way.

People say that when a candidate cares only about the swing states, they ignore the rest of the country. They think the popular vote is a fairer way to make sure candidates divide their attention equally.

Know the Facts!

In 2016, a report from PBS *NewsHour* said that both Donald Trump and Hillary Clinton spent most of their campaign time in the four swing states with the most electoral votes: Florida, Pennsylvania, Ohio, and North Carolina.

The states in purple on this map are the ones that are almost always seen as swing states. The red states' electors often vote Republican, and the blue states' electors often vote for Democrats.

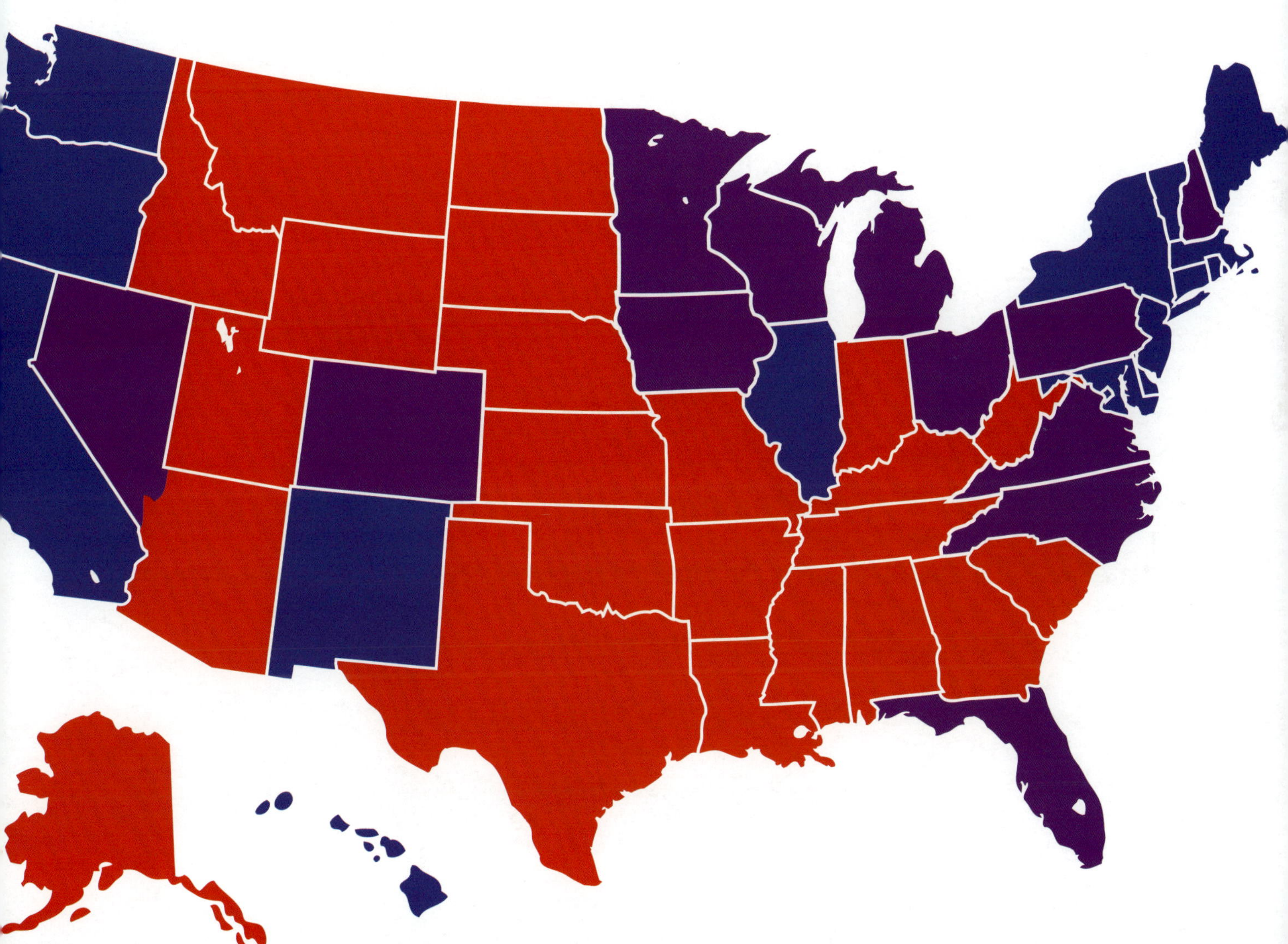

A Clear DECISION

Supporters of the Electoral College say it's important because it makes the winner of a presidential election clear. They believe having a clear winner of presidential elections is part of why democracy works in the United States.

If the United States didn't have the Electoral College, the popular vote might sometimes be too close to call. Then, people would waste a lot of time recounting the votes or having a second election to see who really won. With the Electoral College, there's a clear winner every time: the person who gets at least 270 electoral votes.

Know the Facts!

A president has won the electoral vote but lost the popular vote only five times in U.S. history as of 2019. Many people say this proves the system works well.

In 2000, the presidential race between George W. Bush (left) and Al Gore (right) came down to who won the electoral votes in Florida. The popular vote was so close in that state that it took five weeks of recounts before Bush was announced the winner.

Ignoring the PEOPLE

Many people feel that because of the Electoral College, their vote doesn't count. Republicans who live in blue states and Democrats who live in red states complain that they know the candidate they support won't win even before they vote. For this reason, a lot of people don't bother voting at all. Also, when a candidate wins the popular vote but loses the electoral vote, people say this shows that what the voters wanted doesn't matter.

Many people say that having an election that's decided by the popular vote would **encourage** more citizens to vote. It would give a larger number of people a say in who gets to be president.

Know the Facts!

According to a 2016 poll, fewer than half of Americans think their vote counts.

In the 2016 election, Donald Trump won the electoral vote even though Hillary Clinton won almost 2.9 million more votes than Trump did. Many people believed such a large difference in the number of votes showed the problems with the Electoral College.

Looking at the ARGUMENTS

Some people think the Electoral College is a good system, even if it's not perfect. They think it does a good job of making sure the person who becomes president is the one the **majority** of American people want. Others think it might have been a good system once, but it's not anymore. These people say it isn't fair that someone can lose the popular vote but win the electoral vote.

Now that you know both sides of the argument, what do you think? Does the United States need the Electoral College now?

Know the Facts!

The United States is the only country in the world where people vote for electors to choose the country's leader.

Is the Electoral College necessary?

YES

- It's what the Founding Fathers wanted.
- It's supposed to be fair so the right person for the job is elected.
- Without it, candidates would spend too much time campaigning in cities and ignore smaller communities.
- It makes sure there's a clear winner.

NO

- A lot has changed since the Founding Fathers' time.
- Electors vote for their political party's candidate rather than the right person for the job.
- With it, candidates spend too much time campaigning in swing states and ignore the rest of the states.
- It's possible for a candidate to lose the popular vote but win the electoral vote.

It's important to understand how voting works because it's part of being an active citizen!

GLOSSARY

candidate: A person who runs in an election.

constitution: The basic laws by which a country, state, or group is governed.

encourage: To try to win over to a cause or action.

informed: Having knowledge or facts about something.

majority: More than half.

political party: A group whose members hold the same general beliefs about how government should work.

poll: A sample of the public's opinion on an issue taken by questioning a group of people meant to represent a certain population.

representative: A person who does something on behalf of another person or group.

For More INFORMATION

WEBSITES

Infographic: The Electoral College
online.kidsdiscover.com/infographic/the-electoral-college
This free downloadable infographic gives a step-by-step breakdown of how the Electoral College works.

270 to Win
www.270towin.com
This interactive website allows users to create their own projection of who will win upcoming elections.

BOOKS

Edwards, Sue Bradford. *The Debate About the Electoral College*. Lake Elmo, MN: Focus Readers, 2018.

Grayson, Robert. *Voters: From Primaries to Decision Night*. Minneapolis, MN: Lerner Publishing Group, 2016.

Hunt, Santana. *What Is the Electoral College?*. New York, NY: Gareth Stevens Publishing, 2018.

INDEX